OCS Study MMS 2006-14

Demographics and Behavior of Polar Bears Feeding on Bowhead Whale Carcasses at
Barter and Cross Islands, Alaska,
2002-2004

Prepared for:
U.S. Department of the Interior
Minerals Management Service
Alaska Outer Continental Shelf Region

Final Report
Demographics and Behavior of Polar Bears Feeding on Bowhead Whale Carcasses at
Barter and Cross Islands, Alaska,
2002-2004

by
Susanne Miller, Scott Schliebe, and Kelly Proffitt
U.S. Fish and Wildlife Service
Marine Mammals Management
1011 E. Tudor Road
Anchorage, Alaska 99503

April 2006

This study was funded by the U.S. Department of the Interior, Minerals Management Service, Alaska Outer Continental Shelf Region, Anchorage, Alaska, under Intra-agency Agreement No. 0102RU85166, NSL # AK-02-10, as part of the MMS Alaska Environmental Studies Program.

The opinions, findings, conclusions, or recommendations expressed in this report or product are those of the authors and do not necessarily reflect the views of the U.S. Department of the Interior, nor does mention of trade names or commercial products constitute endorsement or recommendation for use by the Federal Government.

Acknowledgements

The authors wish to thank the Minerals Management Service for funding this study. Special appreciation is extended to the Nuiqsut Whaling Captains Association and the Arctic National Wildlife Refuge for providing accommodations and logistical support at Cross and Barter islands, respectively.

We thank the following people who participated in data collection: Sherman Anderson (Alaska Nanuuq Commission); Anthony Fischbach and Steven Partridge (U.S. Geological Survey, Alaska Science Center); Jason Ransom (National Park Service, Denali National Park), Alan Brackney, Sara Gillespie, Steven Kendall, Jennifer Reed, Cashell Villa, Tara Wertz, and Gary Wheeler (U.S. Fish and Wildlife Service, Arctic National Wildlife Refuge); and Thomas Evans, Craig Perham, Jonathan Snyder, and James Wilder (U.S. Fish and Wildlife Service, Marine Mammals Management). We thank Steven Amstrup, George Durner, and Geoffrey York (U.S. Geological Survey, Alaska Science Center) for providing information on collared bears. Shaylin Howlin (West. Inc.) provided valuable review and guidance on study design. Jeffrey Bromaghin (U.S. Fish and Wildlife Service, Fisheries and Habitat Conservation), Thomas Evans, and Geoffrey York provided useful comments on the draft report.

We are in gratitude to the residents of Kaktovik and Nuiqsut, the Alaska Nanuuq Commission, and the North Slope Borough Department of Wildlife Management for their support of this project.

Table of Contents

List of Tables

List of Figures

Introduction

Background

In the southern Beaufort Sea region, polar bears feed primarily on ringed seals *(Phoca hispida)* and to a lesser extent on bearded seals *(Erignathus barbatus)* (Stirling and Archibald 1977, Smith 1980, Stirling 2002). Polar bears also feed on whale carcasses stranded along the Alaskan coastline during fall months (Craig George, unpublished data, Kalxdorff 1997). In 1999, the U.S. Fish and Wildlife Service (FWS) began flying aerial surveys along the Beaufort Sea coastline between Cape Halkett and Jago Spit near Barter Island (Figure 1) during the fall open water period (September-October) to determine the distribution and abundance of polar bears in the central Beaufort Sea coastal area. Results indicate that the majority (73%) of polar bears observed in 2000-2004 were located within 12 km of Barter Island, where unused portions of bowhead whales *(Balaena mysticetus)* were deposited by Kaktovik residents during fall whaling (14th Polar Bear Specialist Group [PBSG] proceedings, in prep.). Preliminary findings from a 2003 polar bear diet study indicate that bowhead whales comprise part of some bears' diets, based on the stable carbon and nitrogen isotopic composition found in red blood cells obtained from 49 free ranging polar bears (Bentzen et al. 2004). Availability of bowhead whale remains may be a contributing factor to polar bear abundance along coastal areas of the Beaufort Sea (14th PBSG proceedings, in prep, Traditional Ecological Knowledge provided by Kaktovik and Nuiqsut hunters for this study 2005, U.S. Fish and Wildlife Service 1986).

Barter Island is located 145 km west of the Canadian border and within the Arctic National Wildlife Refuge (NWR). Barter Island has been used by Alaska Natives as a traditional gathering place for centuries; the contemporary community of Kaktovik was incorporated as a second class city in 1971. The population of Kaktovik was 293 residents in 2000, most of whom are Native (U.S. Census Bureau 2000). Bowhead whale hunting has been and continues to be an important part of the local culture and lifestyle (Jacobson and Wentworth 1982). Recent fall bowhead whale harvests were first recorded at Kaktovik in 1964; since 1989, two to four whales have been harvested annually (Koski et al. 2005). The majority (64%) of whales are taken between September 1 and 20 (Koski et al. 2005). In recent years, a significant trend towards earlier harvest has occurred, probably because of improved hunting techniques and equipment, and perhaps also because the size of the bowhead population is increasing, and whales may be more numerous near Kaktovik early in the hunting season (Koski et al. 2005).

Cross Island, located approximately 20 km off shore from Prudhoe Bay, serves as the base for Inupiat whalers from Nuiqsut, a small village of approximately 433 residents (U.S. Census Bureau 2000) located approximately 25 km inland from the mouth of the Colville River. Cross Island has been used traditionally and more contemporarily as part of Nuiqsut hunters' traditional subsistence harvest area (BLM 2005). Consistent annual use of Cross Island began around 1986, after a whaler's agreement was signed between Nuiqsut residents and the oil and gas industry. Since then, zero to four whales have been harvested near Cross Island annually (North Slope Borough, unpublished data; M. Galginaitis, pers. comm.). The fall whaling season occurs between late August and early October, depending on ice and weather conditions (BLM 2005).

Whale remains may provide an additional source of nutrition to polar bears immediately prior to onset of winter, a critical time for polar bears, especially pregnant females. However, the potential of whale remains to attract large numbers of polar bears in close proximity to human settlements is of concern because of the likelihood of increased bear-human interactions. High densities of bears may also make animals more vulnerable to other perturbations such as exposure to contaminants and toxic wastes, and to an increased level of disease transmission.

The near shore environment is subject to oil and gas development and other human activities that have the potential to impact polar bears and their foraging habits or activity patterns. Modeling estimates of oil potentially spilled from Outer Continental Shelf (OCS) developments would be improved if information regarding polar bear aggregations along the Beaufort Sea coast during fall months were considered.

Purpose

In 2002 the Minerals Management Service (MMS) provided funds to FWS to conduct a study of polar bears feeding on bowhead whale carcasses along the Beaufort Sea coast of Alaska. The primary purpose of this study was to increase understanding of foraging and carcass utilization by polar bears using the near shore environment. The resulting information has the potential to minimize disturbance to feeding bears from oil and gas development and other human activities. The specific objectives of this study were to:

1) determine the demographics (number, age, and sex) of polar bears using Barter Island during fall months;
2) determine the demographics of polar bears using Cross Island during fall months;
3) determine polar bear behavior (activity patterns) and habitat use at Barter and Cross islands; and
4) determine the magnitude of interchange of polar bears between Barter and Cross islands during fall months.

This information is for use by MMS and other natural resource managers in environmental assessments for oil and gas lease sales, exploration and development projects, oil spill contingency planning, and future bear-human interactions. The information is consistent with and supports conservation of polar bears and their habitats, as mandated under the Marine Mammal Protection Act, and as set forth in the *Habitat Conservation Strategy for Polar Bears in Alaska* (U.S. Fish and Wildlife Service 1995).

Methods

Funding and Participants

Funding was provided in 2002 for a two-year period; in 2003, a modification to the initial contract extended the duration of the study to allow for completion of a third year of field work in 2004.

Polar bears evoke considerable public interest in their conservation and research. In Alaska, a number of entities and organizations both influence and/or are affected by conservation efforts. To facilitate coordination with these entities FWS worked cooperatively with the Alaska Nanuuq Commission (ANC), Alaska Eskimo Whaling Commission (AEWC), North Slope Borough (NSB), and the Native villages of Kaktovik and Nuiqsut prior to and during implementation of this study. The ANC, U.S. Geological Survey's Alaska Science Center (USGS/ASC), and the Arctic NWR provided staff to participate in the study. The Arctic NWR provided accommodations at Barter Island. The Nuiqsut Whaling Captain's Association provided advice, logistical support, and accommodations on Cross Island. The Native Villages of Kaktovik and Nuiqsut worked cooperatively with the FWS to implement a traditional ecological knowledge (TEK) study that provided historical background information on polar bear feeding at Barter and Cross islands. In addition, FWS scheduled annual visits to Kaktovik and Nuiqsut to provide status reports to local residents at public meetings, and to discuss progress of the study with city and tribal councils.

Study Area

The study area lies within the core activity area of the Southern Beaufort Sea population of polar bears (Amstrup 2000, Figure 1). Within this area, Barter and Cross islands were selected, based on prior knowledge of frequent polar bear seasonal habitat use and the reliable presence of bowhead whale remains (Figure 2). At Barter Island (Figure 3) two study sites were selected for monitoring, based on the distribution and activity patterns of bears, as determined by local knowledge and prior reconnaissance. The sites were: 1) Bernard Spit: a barrier island located between 70.08° N 143.36° W and 70.07° N 143.25° W, and a 100 m zone of marine habitat on the near shore (lagoon) side of this area (note that Bernard Spit is used by polar bears primarily for resting, thereby providing the opportunity to observe polar bears at a "non-feeding" site); and 2) Barter Island feeding site ("bone pile"): located approximately 2 km east of the village of Kaktovik. It includes a spit of land on which the bone pile is located, and a 100 m zone of marine habitat surrounding this area. Bernard Spit and the feeding site are separated by Bernard Harbor, a distance of 1-2 km.

Cross Island (Figure 4) is a small (5 km), crescent-shaped barrier island located approximately 20 km off shore from Prudhoe Bay at 70.30° N 147.55° W and is used seasonally by polar bears for both resting and feeding. The Cross Island feeding site includes the bone pile, jawbones, and a 300 m zone around these areas.

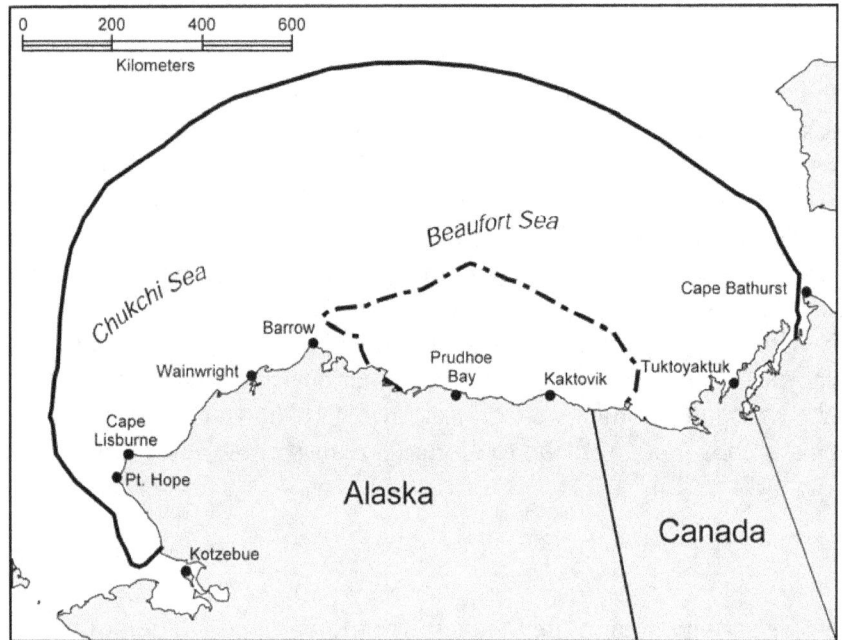

Figure 1. Approximate boundary of the Beaufort Sea polar bear population (solid line) and core activity area (dotted line) as determined by harmonic mean analysis of satellite radio telemetry data collected during 1985-1993 (Amstrup 2000).

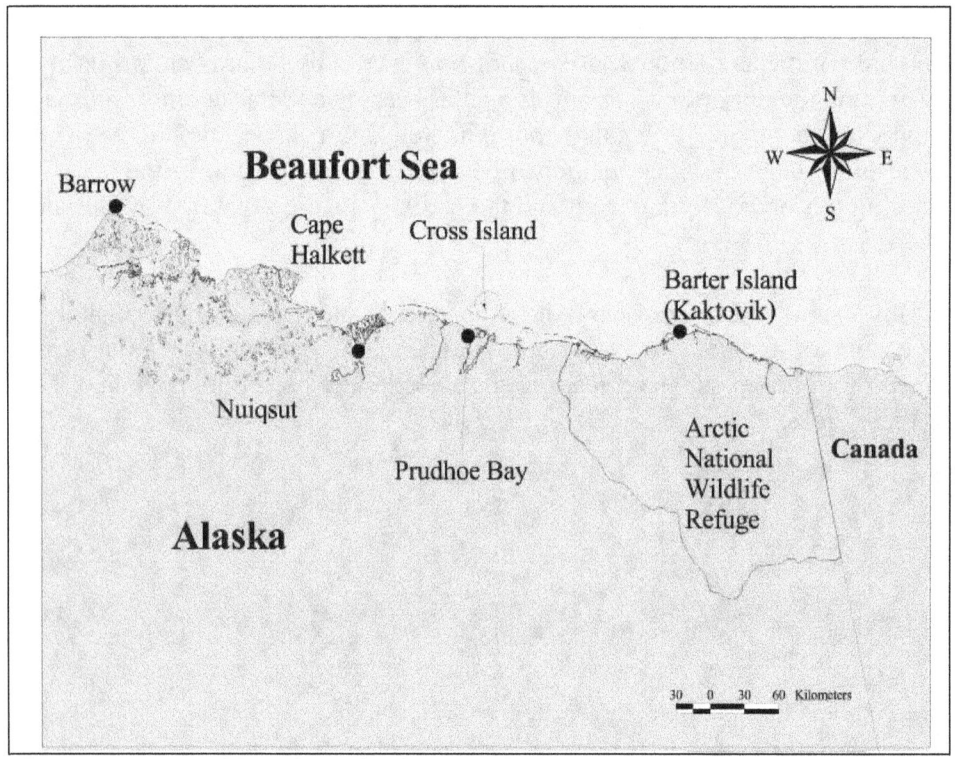

Figure 2. General location of polar bear feeding ecology study area, Alaska, 2002-2004.

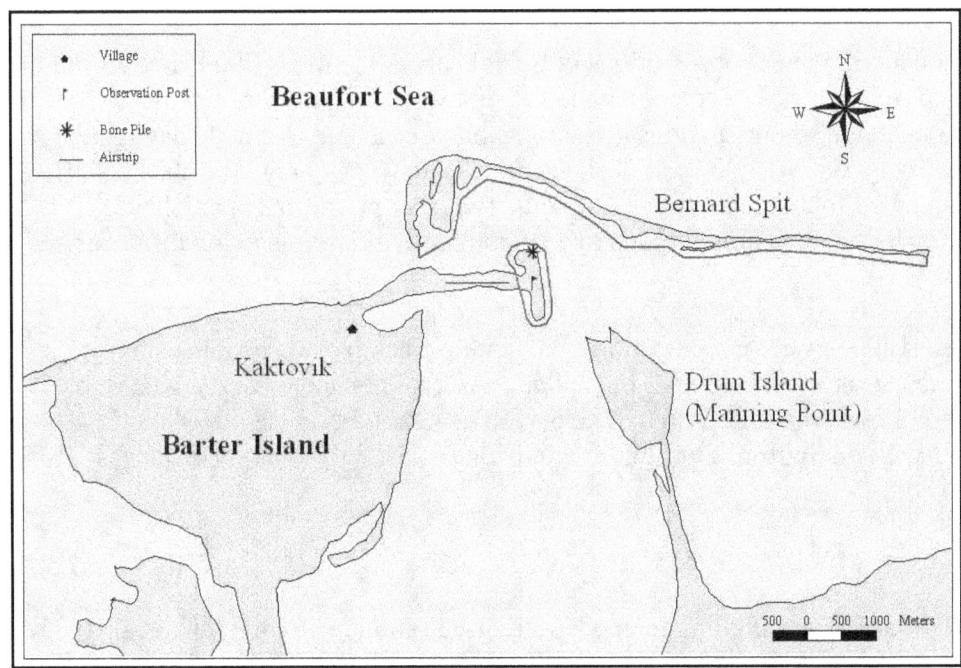

Figure 3. Polar bear feeding ecology study sites at Barter Island, Alaska, 2002-2004.

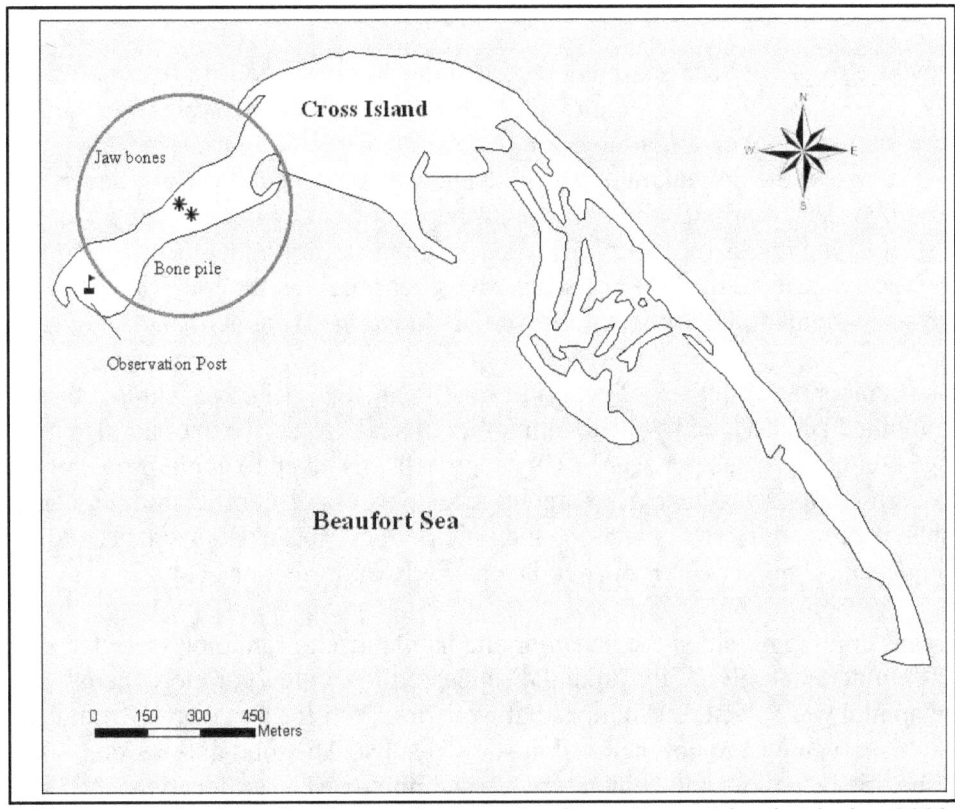

Figure 4. Polar bear feeding ecology study site at Cross Island, Alaska, 2002-2004.

Study Design

Methods involved conducting direct observations of polar bears at the three study sites during the fall open water period between early September and the first week of October. Each 24-hour period was divided into eight 3-hour sessions (= sample units), based on available daylight: 1) dawn (6:00-9:00 h); 2) day (9:00-18:00 h) 3) dusk (18:00-21:00 h); or 4) night (21:00-6:00 h). We systematically sampled four sessions every 24 hours (weather permitting) per island. Bernard Spit could not be sampled at night, due to a combination of large viewing distances and insufficient light.

At Barter Island, observations were conducted from a pick-up truck by two people using Leica Televid 77 spotting scopes and Leitz 10 x 42 binoculars. At Cross Island, observations were conducted from the roof of a whaling cabin by one person using a Leica Televid 77 spotting scope and Smith and Wesson Startron Starlight night vision optics. Observation distances ranged from 10-1000 m.

Sampling Methods

A combination of focal and scan sampling methods were used (Altman 1974, Tacha et al. 1985). Scan sampling data were recorded on data sheets and later entered into a Microsoft Access database. Focal sampling data were recorded using a palmtop computer and The Observer software (Noldus Technology, Leesburg, VA).

Scan Sampling (Study Site Counts). Scan sampling recorded the number, age, and sex of all polar bears observed at the study sites at 15-minute intervals (or 30-minute intervals when large numbers of bears necessitated a longer count interval). Age/sex classes of polar bears were determined based on the size of the animal, number of dependents, presence of collars, and other distinguishing factors, e.g. scars, markings, body size and shape, presence of penile hairs. Animals bearing distinguishing marks (e.g. a collar) were assigned an individual identification number and their presence was noted during each scan; whenever possible, their arrival and departure times were also recorded. Dependent cubs were included in all counts.

During analysis, data (number, age, and sex of bears) from all scans that occurred within a three-hour session were combined and divided by the total number of scans to derive one sample unit per session (= average number of bears per scan). This approach was taken to avoid problems associated with auto-correlation (same bears showing up repeatedly at adjacent 15-minute scans). Sample units were then combined by year, location, and time period. These data were used to derive Study Site Counts and *Age/Sex Composition* data in the **Results** section.

Focal Sampling. Focal sampling recorded the behavior and habitat use of randomly-selected polar bears during 20-minute intervals. If the animal disappeared from view for more than five minutes, a new focal animal was selected. Animals that were observed for less than ten minutes before they became unobservable were not included in study results. The total number of minutes engaged in specific behaviors and habitat type was combined by year, location, and time period for analysis. Bear behavior and habitat types are defined in **Appendix 1.**

Whole Island Counts. In addition to sampling effort at the study sites, we obtained daily counts of the number of polar bears visible at Barter and Cross islands. At Barter Island, this included all observable terrestrial areas, (including the two study sites), Kaktovik Lagoon, Bernard Harbor, and Drum Island. At Cross Island, whole island counts included numbers of animals that were present anywhere on the island, including the feeding site. Dependent cubs were included in all counts.

TEK. Representatives from the Native Villages of Kaktovik and Nuiqsut (tribal councils) conducted meetings with ten residents (seven from Kaktovik, three from Nuiqsut) to discuss historical use of bowhead whale carcasses. Their observations were recorded on data collection forms and later summarized by village; some of the information was included in this report.

The following assumptions are inherent to the study plan: 1) sampling protocols adequately document patterns of use with respect to time during the study period; and 2) observers are capable of categorizing bears into appropriate age/sex classes, recognizing that some animals cannot be classified to age or sex due to a lack of distinguishing physical features, or to restricted visibility.

Results

Monitoring Effort

The study period occurred annually between September 3 and October 4, 2002-2004 (Table 1). A total of 1,230 hours of observations were conducted, including 4,733 scans and 926 focal samples. Overall, monitoring effort was allocated as follows: 44% at the Barter Island feeding site; 40% at Cross Island, and 16% at Bernard Spit.

Table 1. Monitoring effort for polar bear feeding ecology study at Barter and Cross islands, Alaska, September/October, 2002-2004.

	Barter Island			Cross Island		
	2002	**2003**	**2004**	**2002**	**2003**	**2004**
Study Period	Sep. 3-29	Sep. 8-Oct. 3	Sep. 9-Oct. 4	Sep. 10-25	Sep. 15-27	Sep. 16-27
# Hours Monitored	209	247	277	184	170	144
# Scan Samples	739	831	1085	770	714	594
# Focal Samples	213	229	290	23	38	133

Number of Polar Bears at Barter and Cross Islands

Whole Island Counts. We observed a range of 0-65 bears within the Barter Island study area, with a 3-year mean of 33.1 (SD= 15.5) bears. At the Cross Island study area, we observed a range of 0-13 bears with a 3-year mean of 6.1 (SD=3.8) bears (Table 2).

Table 2. Estimated number of polar bears observed during "whole island" counts at Barter and Cross islands, Alaska, 2002-2004.

	Barter Island			Cross Island		
	2002	2003	2004	2002	2003	2004
Study Period	Sept. 3-29	Sept. 8-Oct. 3	Sept. 9-Oct. 4	Sept. 10-25	Sept. 15-27	Sept. 16-27
# of Counts	22	33	28	16	13	50
Minimum # of Bears	0	3	22	0	1	4
Maximum # of Bears	51	61	65	7	7	13
Mean # of Bears	22.8	33.6	40.6	1.5	3	8.4
Standard Deviation (SD)	17.7	14.3	9.7	2	2	2.3
3-Year Mean ± SD	33.1 ± 15.5			6.1 ± 3.8		

Study Site Counts. At Bernard Spit, we observed a range of 3-61 bears with a 3-year mean of 27.7 (SD= 10.1) bears. At the Barter Island feeding site, we observed a range of 0-37 bears with a 3-year mean of 4.9 (SD= 4.9) bears. At Cross Island, we observed a range of 0-12 bears with a 3-year mean of 2.8 (SD = 2.7) bears. The minimum, maximum and mean number of polar bears observed annually at the selected study sites is described in Table 3.

Table 3. Estimated number of polar bears observed at study sites on Barter and Cross islands, Alaska, 2002-2004.

	Bernard Spit			Barter Island Feeding Site			Cross Island Feeding Site		
	2002	2003	2004	2002	2003	2004	2002	2003	2004
Study Period	Sep. 3-29	Sep. 8 Oct. 3	Sep. 9 Oct. 4	Sep. 10-25	Sep. 15-27	Sep. 16-27	Sep. 11-25	Sep. 15-27	Sep. 16-27
# of Scans	84	191	201	655	640	884	463	516	553
Minimum # Bears	3	10	9	0	0	0	0	0	0
Maximum # Bears	44	61	48	37	29	34	4	6	12
Mean # Bears	25.4	31.8	25.1	6.2	4.7	4.1	0.5	1.6	5.6
Standard Deviation (SD)	10.9	10.2	7.5	5.3	5.2	4.0	0.8	1.3	2.1
3-Year Mean ± SD	27.7 ± 10.1			4.9 ± 4.9			2.8 ± 2.7		

We analyzed data by time period to determine whether time of day had an effect on bear numbers present at the feeding sites (Table 4). At Barter Island, the highest period of use was at "night" at the feeding site with an average of 8 polar bears per scan, compared to 3 and < 1 polar bears/scan during "dawn/dusk" and "day" periods respectively. During the "day" period, most polar bears had moved from the feeding site to off-shore areas such as Bernard Spit and Drum Island. An average of 30 polar bears/scan were observed at Bernard Spit during the day, compared to 25 during dawn/dusk when bears were more active (see also <u>Behavior</u> section). Night use of Bernard Spit is unknown since the area was not visible to observers. At Cross Island, bear use of the feeding site was similar during "day" and "dawn/dusk" time periods with an average of 3 polar bears per scan. No reliable estimates were obtained for the "night" period because of restricted visibility, despite the use of night-vision optics. We know polar bears were active at night as evidenced by numerous bears encountered in close proximity to our observation post; however, we were unable to quantify the extent to which they were present at the feeding site.

Table 4. Estimated number of polar bears observed during day, dawn/dusk, and night at study sites, 2002-2004.

	Bernard Spit		BTI Feeding Site		Cross Island	
Time Period	Mean	SD	Mean	SD	Mean	SD
Day	29.5	10.2	0.9	1.4	3.1	2.8
Dawn/Dusk	25.3	9.6	3.3	2.4	2.5	2.6
Night	---	---	8.3	5.0	---	---

<u>Brown Bears.</u> Of special interest was the presence of 8-12 brown bears (*Ursus arctos*) at the Barter Island feeding site in 2003 and 2004. While polar and brown bears have been observed interacting at the Prudhoe Bay dump (Richard Shideler and Scott Schliebe, pers. comm.), to our knowledge, these are the first recorded incidents of polar and brown bears interacting at bowhead whale carcasses in Alaska. Additional information on interactions between the two species will be collected at Barter Island in 2005.

Age-Sex Composition

All age-sex classes of polar bears were observed at both Barter and Cross islands during the study period (Figure 5). At the Barter Island feeding site, 47% of the bears observed during the three-year period were comprised of family groups (17% mothers, 30% dependent cubs); 35% were single bears (24% adults, 11% sub-adults); and 18% were bears of unknown age or gender. At Cross Island, 27% of the bears observed were comprised of family groups (12% mothers, 15% cubs); 66% were single bears (63% adults, 3% sub-adults), and 7% were bears of unknown age or gender.

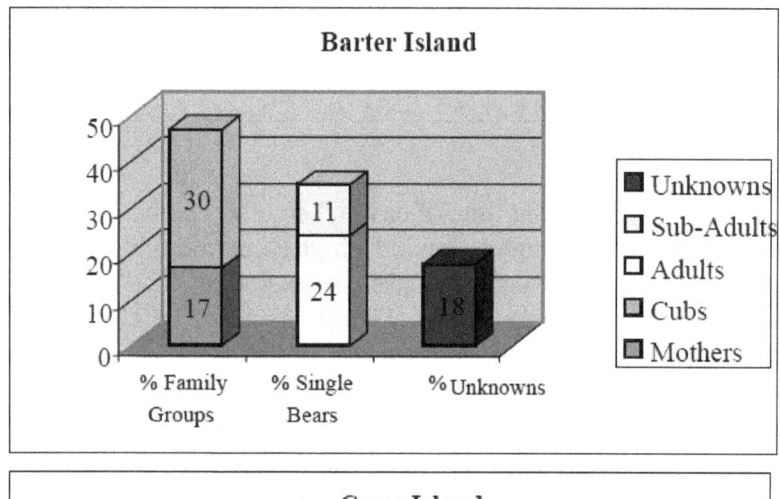

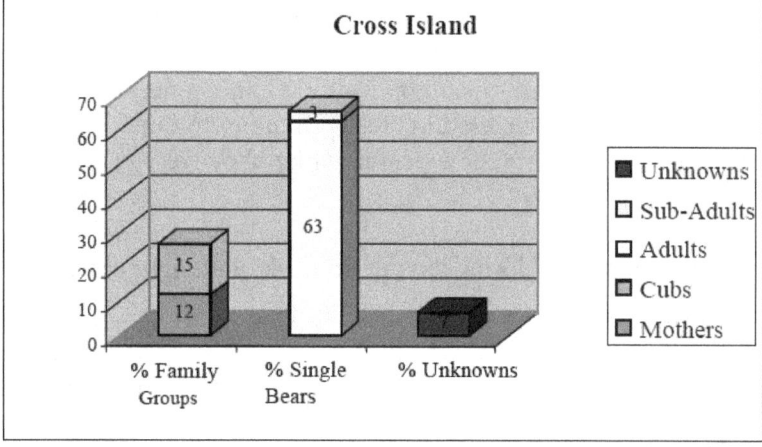

Figure 5. Proportion of polar bear age-sex classes observed at Barter and Cross islands, Alaska, 2002-2004.

We analyzed data by time period to determine whether time of day had an effect on age-sex composition of polar bears at the feeding sites. Age-sex data for Bernard Spit and Cross Island at night were excluded from analyses since extensive viewing distances prevented accurate aging and sexing of animals and resulted in a high proportion of animals being classified as unknowns (= bears of unknown age and gender). At Barter Island, the proportion of family groups and sub-adults was greatest during "day" and "dawn/dusk" time periods, whereas the proportion of single adults was greatest during "night" time periods (Figure 6). Similarly, at Cross Island the proportion of family groups using the feeding site was greater during the "day" time period, whereas the proportion of single adults was greater during the "dawn/dusk" time period.

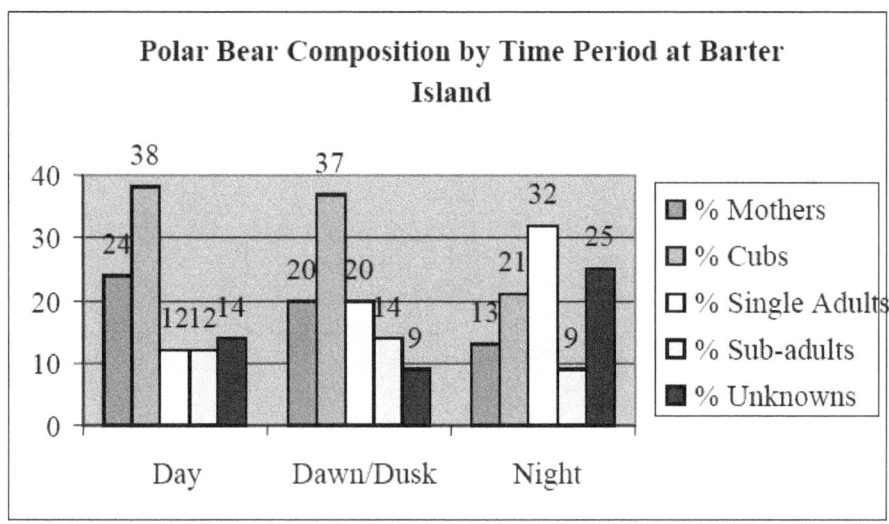

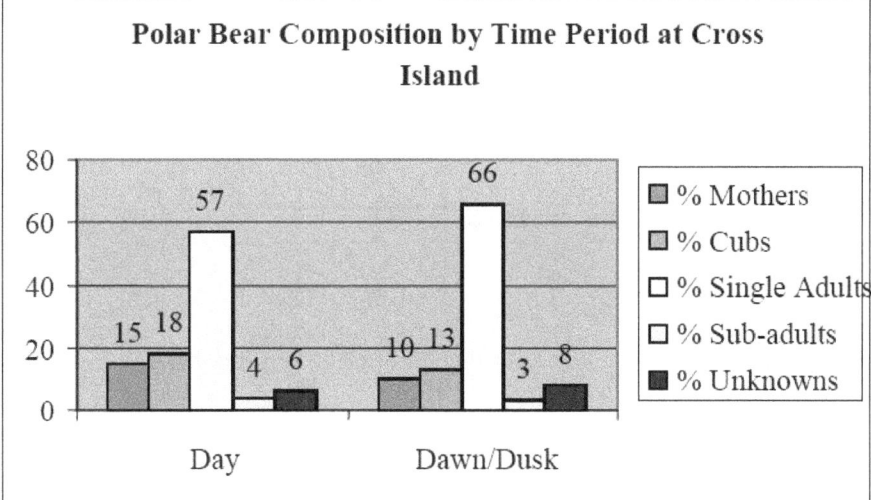

Figure 6. Age-sex composition of polar bears observed at feeding sites on Barter and Cross islands compared by time period, 2002-2004.

Behavior and Activity Patterns

Figure 7 depicts behavior exhibited by polar bears at the study sites during 2002-2004.
Behaviors that constituted less than 1% of the total time were excluded from results; night data
for Cross Island was also excluded from results. A total of 17,670 minutes collected during 911
focal samples were used for these analyses. The predominant behavior at Bernard Spit and Cross
Island was laying (69% and 60% respectively); at the Barter Island feeding site the predominant
activity was feeding (64%).

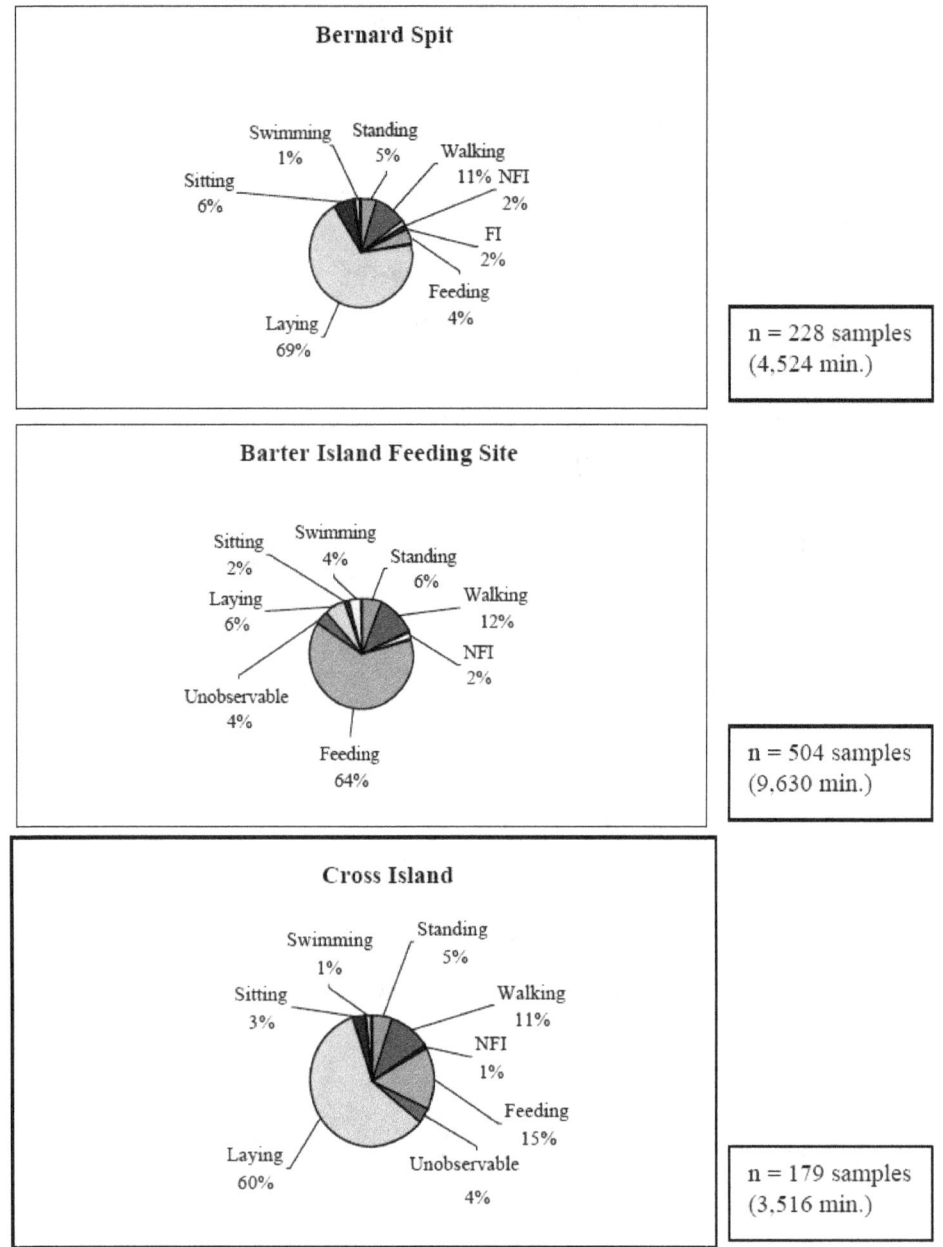

Figure 7. Behavior of polar bears observed on Barter and Cross islands, Alaska, 2002-2004. FI
= family interactions among mothers and dependent cubs; NFI = non-family interactions.

12

When specific behaviors were compared by time period, (Figures 8-10), bears at all study sites during the "day" time periods were predominantly inactive (laying, sitting, or standing) and allocated the least amount of time feeding compared with other time periods. Non-family interactions and walking behaviors were greater during "dawn/dusk" time periods compared to "day" time periods at all study sites. Non-family interactions during "night" time periods were also greater than during the "day" time period at the Barter Island feeding site.

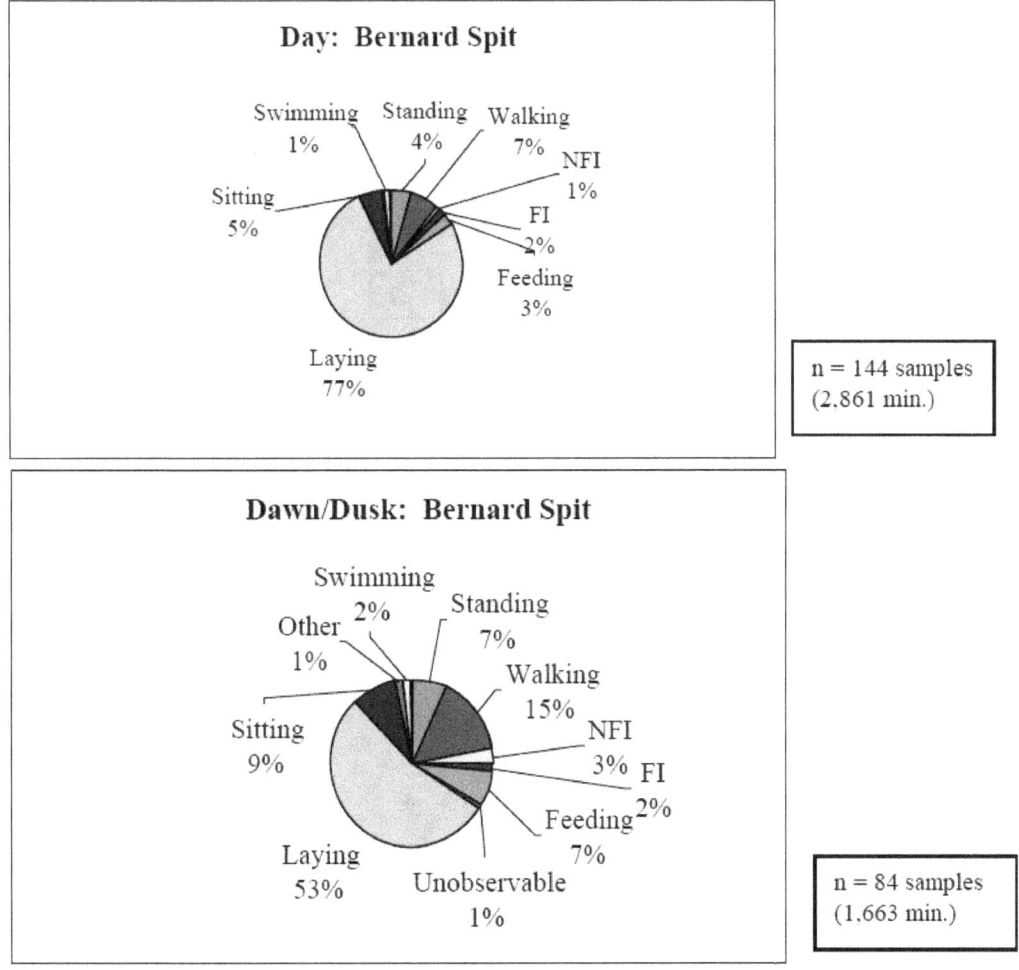

Figure 8. Polar bear behavior compared by time period at Bernard Spit, Alaska 2002-2004. Dawn = 6:00-9:00h; Day = 9:00-18:00h; Dusk = 18:00-21:00h; Night = 21:00-03=06:00h). FI = family interactions among mothers and dependent cubs; NFI = non-family interactions.

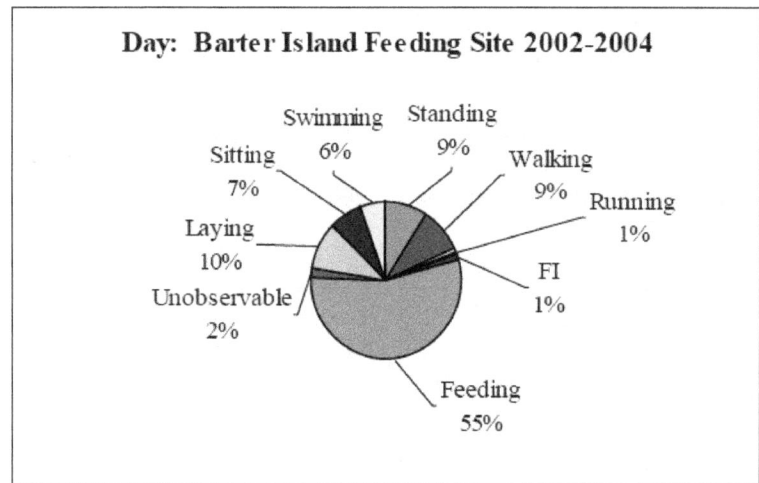

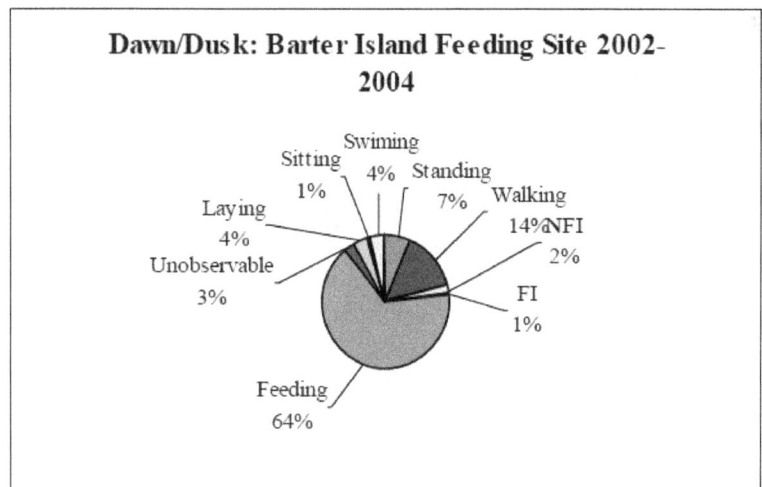

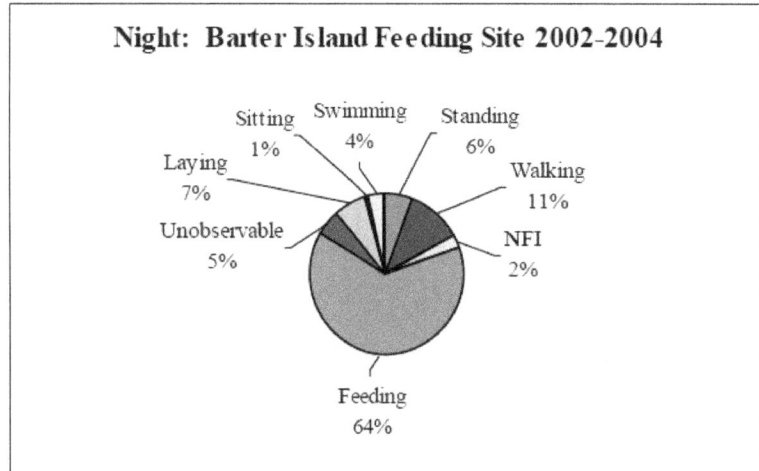

Figure 9. Polar bear behavior compared by time period at the Barter Island feeding site, Alaska, 2002-2004. Dawn = 6:00-9:00h; Day = 9:00-18:00h; Dusk = 18:00-21:00h; Night = 21:00-03=06:00h). FI = family interactions among mothers and dependent cubs; NFI = non-family interactions.

14

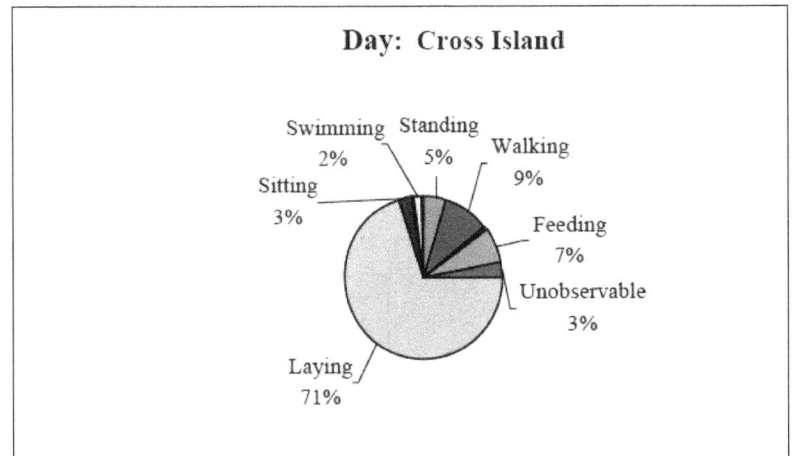

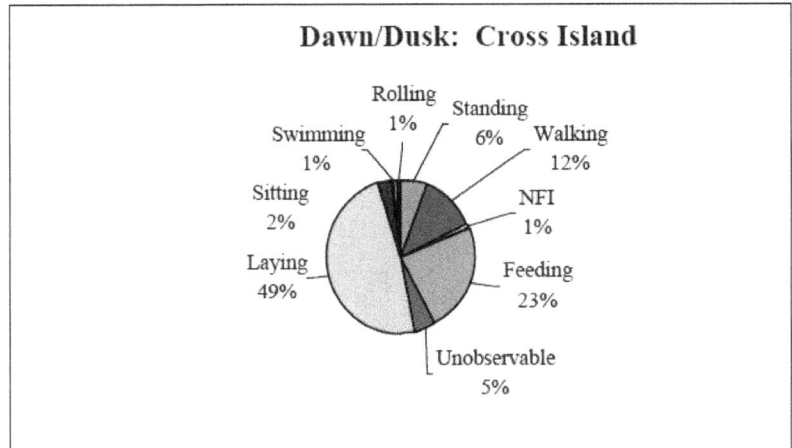

Figure 10. Polar bear behavior compared by time period at Cross Island, Alaska, 2002-2004. Dawn = 6:00-9:00h; Day = 9:00-18:00h; Dusk = 18:00-21:00h; Night = 21:00-03=06:00h). FI = family interactions among mothers and dependent cubs; NFI = non-family interactions.

When specific behaviors were compared by age-sex class (Figures11-13), some differences were noted among cohorts. At Bernard Spit, sub-adult bears spent a greater proportion of time walking, feeding, and engaged in non-family interactions than single adult bears or mothers with cubs. At the Barter Island feeding site, single adult bears spent a greater proportion of time feeding; sub-adult bears spent a greater proportion of time walking; females accompanied by cubs spent a greater proportion of time engaged in standing, sitting, laying, and swimming behaviors than each of their respective cohorts.

15

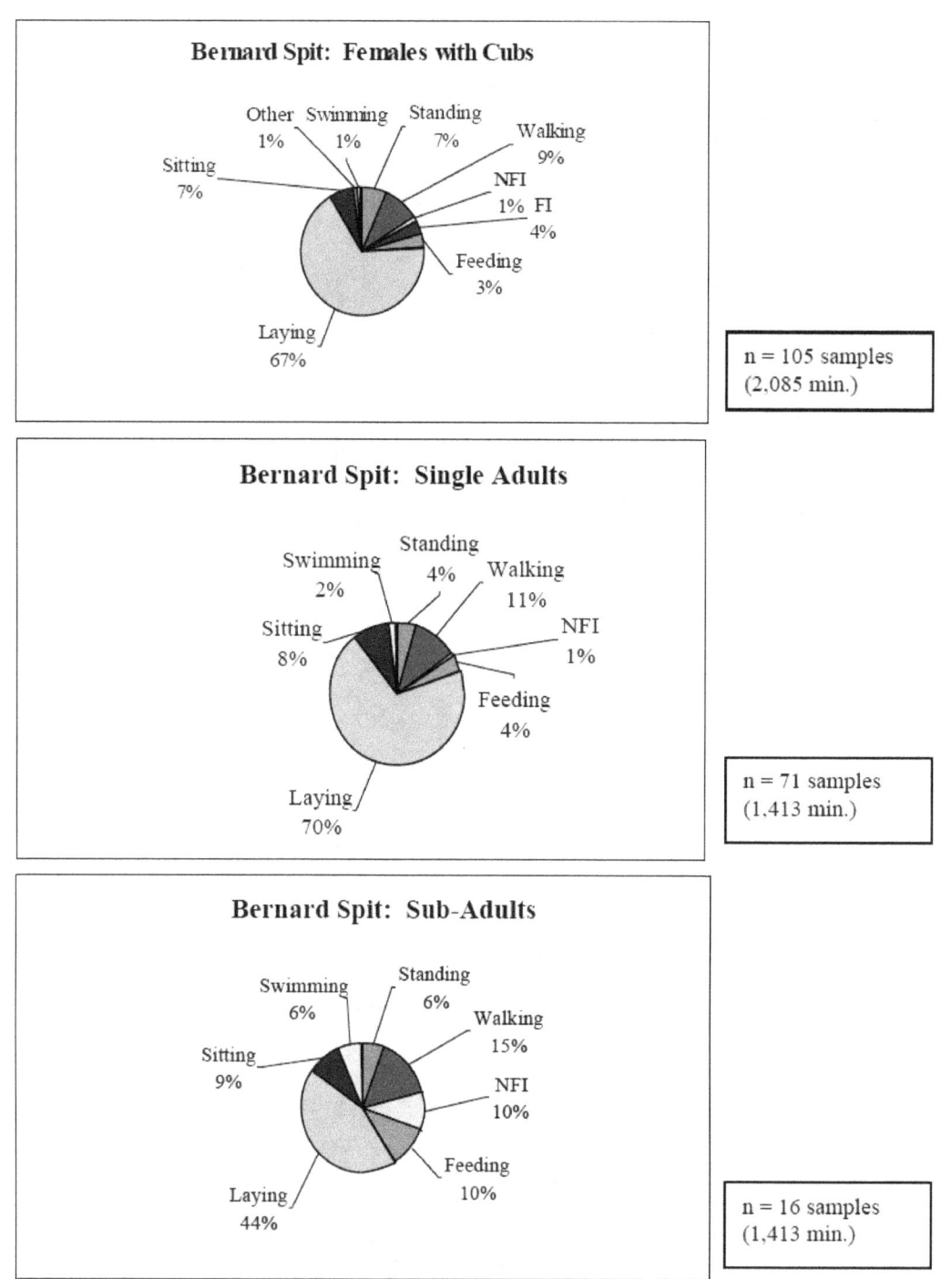

Figure 11. Polar bear behavior compared by age/sex class at Bernard Spit, Alaska, 2002-2004. FI = family interactions among mothers and dependent cubs; NFI = non-family interactions.

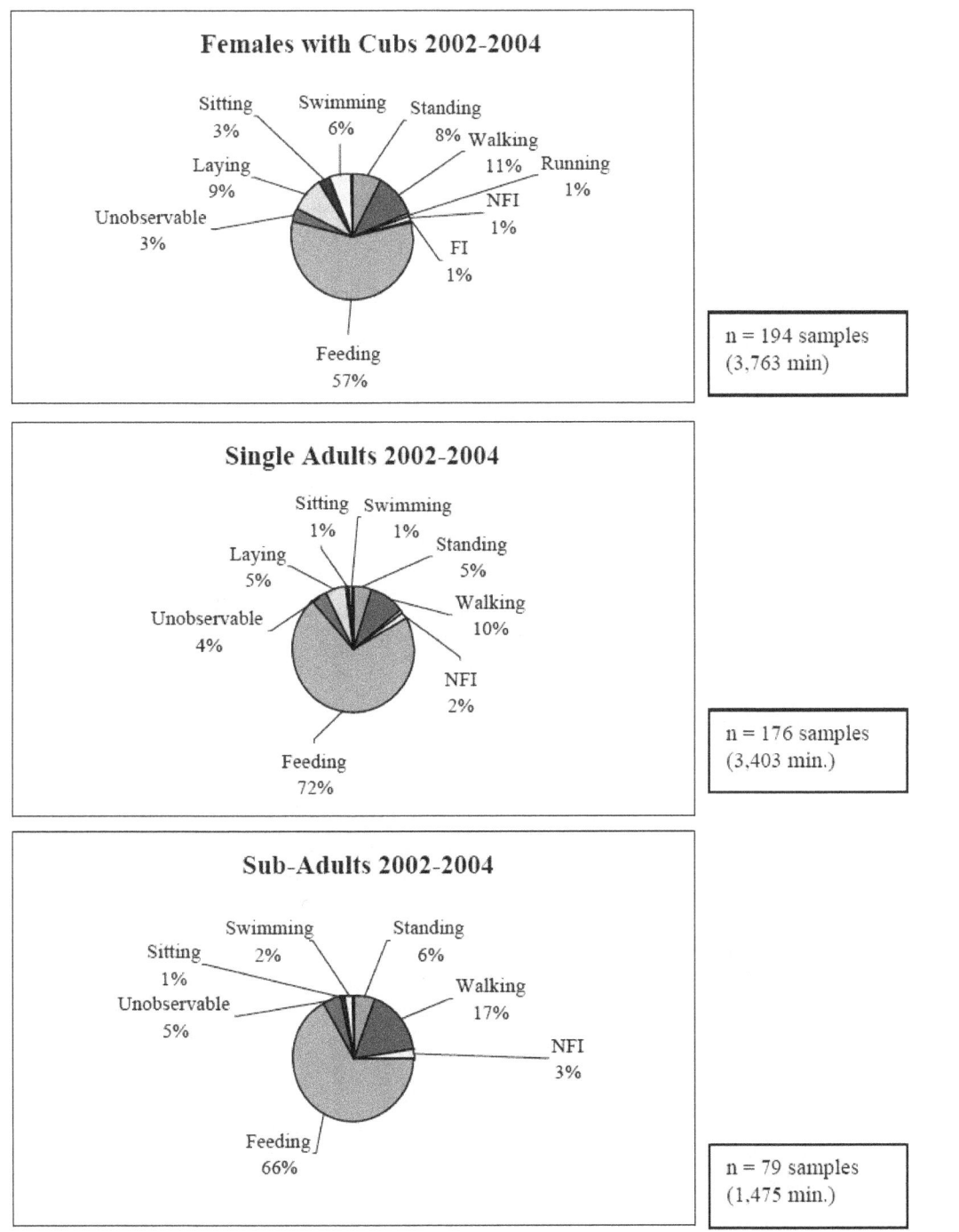

Females with Cubs 2002-2004

- Sitting 3%
- Swimming 6%
- Standing 8%
- Walking 11%
- Running 1%
- NFI 1%
- FI 1%
- Feeding 57%
- Unobservable 3%
- Laying 9%

n = 194 samples (3,763 min)

Single Adults 2002-2004

- Sitting 1%
- Swimming 1%
- Standing 5%
- Walking 10%
- NFI 2%
- Feeding 72%
- Unobservable 4%
- Laying 5%

n = 176 samples (3,403 min.)

Sub-Adults 2002-2004

- Swimming 2%
- Standing 6%
- Sitting 1%
- Walking 17%
- NFI 3%
- Feeding 66%
- Unobservable 5%

n = 79 samples (1,475 min.)

Figure 12. Polar bear behavior compared by age/sex class at the Barter Island feeding site, Alaska, 2002-2004. FI = family interactions among mothers and dependent cubs; NFI = non-family interactions.

At Cross Island, single adults spent the greatest proportion of time laying and the least proportion of time walking; conversely, sub-adults spent the least proportion of time laying and the greatest proportion of time walking and feeding. Females with dependent cubs also spent a greater proportion of time walking than single adults, and a slightly greater proportion of time swimming than either single adult or sub-adult bears.

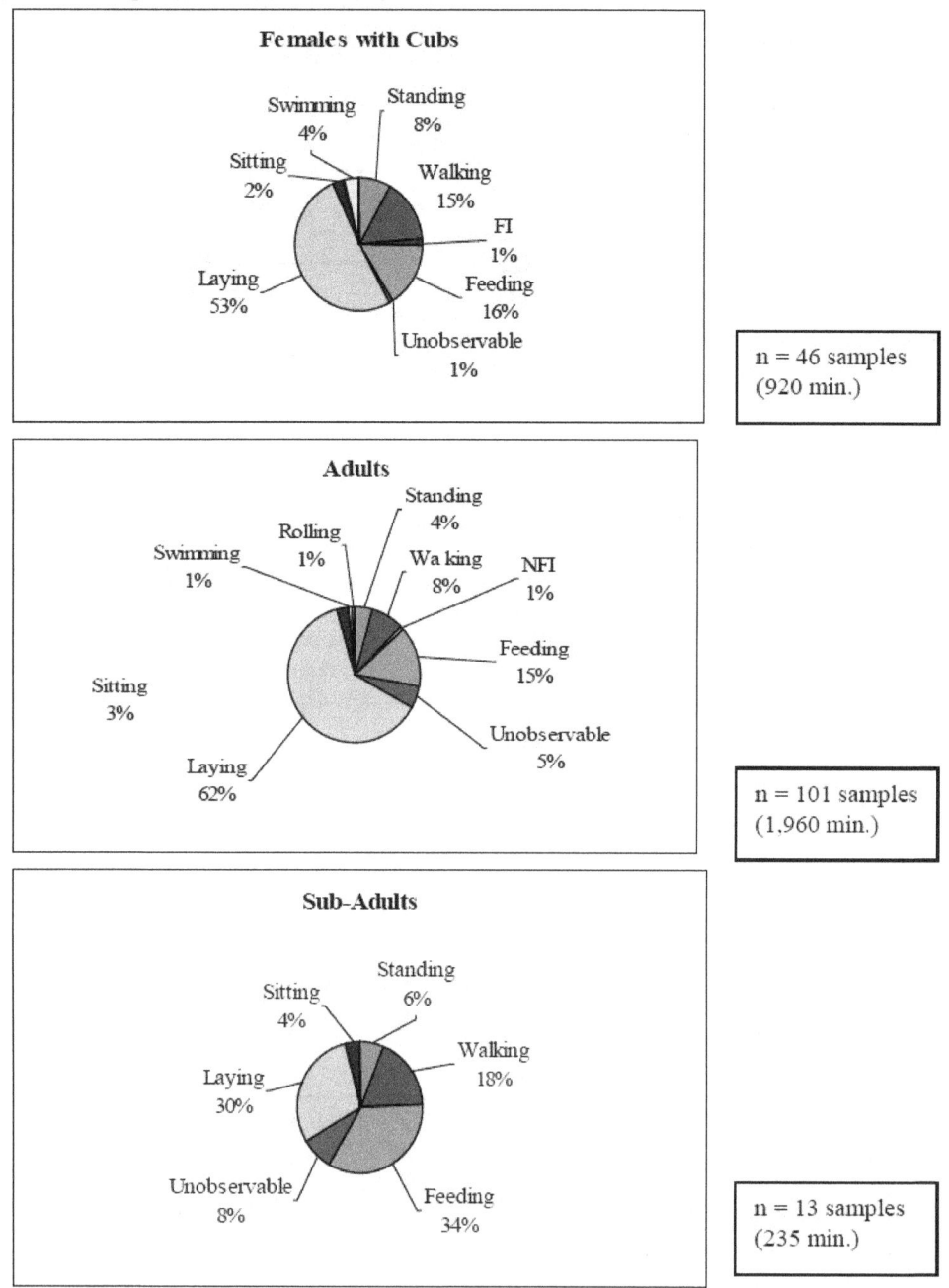

Figure 13. Polar bear behavior compared by age-sex class at Cross Island, Alaska, 2002-2004. FI = family interactions among mothers and dependent cubs; NFI = non-family interactions.

18

Habitat Use

Habitat types used by polar bears during this study were classified as: mainland (Barter Island feeding site); barrier island (Bernard Spit and Cross Island); and marine habitat (marine portions of study sites). In all years the study period ended prior to freeze-up (= formation of ice adjacent to shore); therefore, no use of ice habitat was recorded. Although marine habitat was under-represented as a habitat type at our study sites, we recorded the frequency of its use (as the number of times bears entered water during focal sampling) in an effort to provide information useful in assessing the potential risk of polar bears contacting oil in the marine environment in event of a fuel spill. The question posed was: *once polar bears arrive on the coastline during the fall open water period, do they stay exclusively on land until freeze-up?* Our data indicate that polar bears did not stay exclusively on land; rather, they made use of the marine environment after they arrived at our study sites. At Barter Island, most polar bears accessed and departed from the feeding site by swimming and, based on observations of individually recognizable bears, we believe that most polar bears were using the feeding sites every 1-2 days, although the duration of their stay at the study sites varied (see also ***Movements/Interchange*** section). In addition to arrival and departure, bears at the Barter Island feeding site were observed using marine habitat in 23% (114/504) of focal animal samples and 6% (14/228) of focal animal samples at Bernard Spit.

Marine use at Cross Island was less frequent, probably because once polar bears are on the island, they can access the feeding site from anywhere on the island without having to enter marine habitat each time they want to feed. This is due to the availability of undisturbed resting areas adjacent to the feeding site at Cross Island, and lack of alternative barrier island habitat nearby. Bear use of marine habitat was documented during 4% (7/194) of focal animal samples at Cross Island. In addition to swimming, we observed polar bears walking, standing, interacting, playing (with objects), cleaning fur, and carrying and eating muktuk (small pieces of whale skin with blubber attached) while in marine waters. Females with dependent cubs were the cohort most frequently observed in marine waters at all study sites.

Movements and Interchange of Polar Bears between Barter and Cross Islands

Duration of Residency at Study Sites. We recorded the number of days that individually recognizable polar bears were present at the study sites to determine whether polar bears remained present throughout the study period. Our data suggests that the duration of temporary residency within the immediate area varies by individual. Since we did not monitor the feeding site continuously, it is possible that polar bears fed while we were not present to observe them, and thus remained resident to the area without our knowledge. Table 5 provides sighting and movement information for five individually recognizable polar bears observed in 2002 at Barter Island. These data indicate that some polar bears stay for longer periods, while others may pass through the area more quickly. This variability in duration of residency was also observed at Cross Island. In 2002 and 2003, most polar bears remained on the island for short periods (< 24 h). In 2004, several large males and at least one family group stayed the entire (two-week) study period, yet another family group left after approximately one week.

Table 5. Sighting and telemetry movement information for radio-collared bears observed at Barter Island, Alaska, 2002-2004. ASC = U.S. Geological Survey, Alaska Science Center (responsible for polar bear research and collaring activities). COY= cub of the year (<1 year old).

ASC Bear ID	Life History	Dates Observed at Barter Island	Notes
20564	Adult female, age unknown; accompanied by 2 COYs in 2002	September 7-25, 2002	2002: observed at feeding site every 1-2 days. Telemetry: moved west and then off shore in December 2002. Not known to have used Cross Island. No data available for 2003-2004.
20465	Mature adult female born in 1983; observed with no dependent cubs in 2002	September 8-14, 2002	2002: one observed visit to feeding site in 2002. Telemetry: no telemetry data in 2002-2003; radio locations obtained near Barter Island in May 2004. Not known to have used Cross Island.
20413	Young adult female born in 1997; observed with no dependent cubs in 2002	September 9-19, 2002	2002: visited feeding site on at least 2 occasions. Telemetry: data suggests that home range was in near-shore area in 2002. Located on Cross Island in December 2002. No data available for 2003-2004.
20419	Mature adult female born in 1990; accompanied by 3 COYs in 2002 and 3 yearlings in 2003.	September 18-28, 2002 and September 9 - October 3, 2003	2002: 1 COY smaller than the other two. Visited feeding site every 1-2 days. 2003: 3 yearlings present; visited feeding site every 1-2 days. Telemetry: collar removed in spring 2004. Not known to have used Cross Island.
1737	Mature adult female born in 1970; observed with no dependent cubs in 2002.	September 28, 2002 (last full day of study period)	2002: appeared to be in poor condition and was present at the feeding site for at least 15 hours; departure of observers precluded further quantification of her length of stay. Telemetry: located annually within 10 km of Barter Island feeding site in 1989-1992. Located on Cross Island in December 2002/January 2003.

Interchange of Bears between Barter and Cross Islands. To determine whether polar bears observed at Barter Island also use Cross Island, individually recognizable animals must be followed over time. Research biologists in Alaska routinely capture and outfit polar bears from the southern Beaufort Sea population with satellite radio-collars to track their movements and collect information regarding other aspects of their life history. During the study period we observed ten radio-collared females at our study sites; of these, five had actively transmitting collars and were therefore recognizable as individuals. All five of these bears were observed in

2002 at Barter Island (see Table 5). No radio-collared bears were observed at Cross Island during 2002; thus collared bears observed at Barter Island did not travel to Cross Island during the study period. Similarly, no collared bears were observed on Cross Island in 2003; one collared adult female with 2 COYs was observed on Cross Island in 2004 but her collar was inactive, so we were unable to determine her identity. The distance between Cross and Barter islands is approximately 215 km; the 2-week duration of the study period at Cross Island in combination with the presence of a vast amount of open water during the study period probably limits the possibility of re-sighting individuals at both sites. Anecdotal information from aerial flights and observations of industry personnel working in the Cross Island area leads us to believe that the chronology of use of Cross Island may be later in the year. We reviewed satellite location information provided by USGS/ASC (unpublished data) to determine whether polar bears moved between the islands later in the season. These data suggest that polar bear movement between the two islands can occur after freeze-up, as illustrated by bear ID #1737 and 20413 (Table 5).

Intra-Annual Use of Study Sites. Another question posed to FWS was: *are the same polar bears returning to the feeding site during subsequent years?* Again, results are based on information related to radio-collared bears provided by USGS/ASC. Of the five collared bears that we observed at Barter Island, we know that at least one family group (ASC bear id 20419) visited Barter Island in subsequent years (2002 and 2003) during the open water season. The ASC captured this bear in the spring of 2004 and removed her collar; therefore, it is unknown whether she returned to Barter Island during 2004.

Discussion

Demography of Polar Bears Using Barter and Cross Islands

Number of Polar Bears. Polar bears are believed to be relatively solitary animals unless in family groups, during mating season, or when food sources are concentrated in small areas, such as along leads. In Alaska, some polar bears come to shore during fall months and an increasing trend of use of coastal habitat during the fall open-water period is occurring. Traditional knowledge provided by Kaktovik and Nuiqsut hunters and elders indicates that bear distribution and abundance along the coast is closely related to ice conditions, and that distance of ice from shore affects the numbers of polar bear using the coastline. In 2005, Schliebe et al. (14th PBSG proceedings, in prep.) performed a regression analysis on the relationship between the number of polar bears on shore and distance from shore to the ice pack. They found that, as distance to ice increased, the number of bears increased; conversely, as ice advanced near-shore, the number of bears decreased. Durner et al. (2004) found that several factors, such as the extent of ice cover, ocean depth, and ice form and stage were important in habitat selection by polar bears, and that habitat selection is likely driven by prey availability and accessibility, as well as the availability of safe resting places.

The factors that determine whether a polar bear will remain on sea ice or come to shore during late summer or fall are complex and may also be changing over time. We know that between

2000 and 2004 the majority of polar bears observed along the coast during the fall open water period occurred within 12 km of Barter Island (14th PBSG proceedings, in prep.). Results from this study further confirm that polar bears tend to aggregate on Barter and Cross islands during the fall open water period, with greater bear numbers observed at Barter Island than at Cross Island. While bowhead whale remains may not be the primary reason why polar bears come to shore, these attractants likely play a role in concentrating polar bears that are using coastal areas during fall months.

The feeding sites were used by a mean of 4.9 and 2.8 polar bears per scan at Barter and Cross islands, respectively, during the given study periods (see Table 3). At Cross Island, the mean number of bears using the feeding site increased over the 3-year period, as did numbers of bears using the entire island. However, at Barter Island, the mean number of bears using the bone pile was highest in 2002 and decreased in subsequent years, despite higher numbers of bears in the area. This indicates that local factors such as the quantity of whale remains may influence bear use of the feeding sites. For example, in 2002, Kaktovik whalers struck and lost a whale that was later recovered, but at that point, much of the whale was not suitable for human consumption, and the unused portions were placed at the bone pile. Other factors that may account for fewer bears using the bone pile in 2003 and 2004 include the social dynamics among polar bears, brown bears, and humans. For example, we frequently observed the presence of brown bears displacing polar bears from the feeding site. Further research to quantify such interactions is currently underway.

Another factor that may affect numbers of polar bears using whale remains at Barter and Cross islands is time of day. At Barter Island, bear numbers were greatest at night and less during day. Cross Island night observations were not quantified but anecdotal observations of bears moving around the island (not always within our defined study area), as well as frequent encounters with polar bears at the viewing platform, indicate that activity is greater at night on Cross Island as well.

Age-Sex Composition. All age-sex classes were observed at Barter and Cross islands; a greater proportion of bears were in family groups at Barter Island, whereas a greater proportion of bears were single adults at Cross Island. Age-sex composition data should be interpreted with caution because of the classification of a significant number of "unknown" age-sex animals that, if classified to sex or age, might affect cohort proportions.

We did not expect to see many large adult males at the feeding sites since they have the ability to displace other sex/age classes from preferred feeding habitats out on sea ice. This is further evidenced by an under-representation of adult males in the harvest (Scott Schliebe, pers. comm.). Adult males were observed every year at both Barter and Cross islands during this study. Their presence along the coast might be related to ice conditions, declining seal availability, presence of attractants on shore, or other factors. This subject warrants further investigation.

Behavior. Polar bears generally became more active with the onset of darkness. Study results from Barter Island indicate that polar bears actively feed most frequently at night; since we did not observe all "day" bears at the feeding site at night, some bears must either remain on Bernard

Spit or similar habitat; visit the feeding site when we are not monitoring it, or leave the area.

The increase in non-family bear-bear interactions during "dusk/dawn" at Bernard Spit and Cross Island, and at "night" at the Barter Island feeding site may be related to increased bear densities and activity levels. Given the high number of bears in a relatively small radius area near the feeding sites, surprisingly few aggressive interactions were observed. All age/sex classes of polar bears were often observed feeding simultaneously in close proximity of each other, including large adult males feeding right next to females with dependent cubs. While some bears, particularly females with COYs, seemed to become agitated or even displaced by the presence of other bears, overall, most polar bears seemed to tolerate each other. We also frequently observed large males resting in close proximity of each other, as well as arriving at and departing from the feeding sites together. Aggressive interactions among all polar bears tended to be short in duration and initiated by mothers or curious cubs. More intra-specific aggression may occur if the food supply were more limited. When brown bears were present, they tended to be dominant over polar bears and sometimes displaced polar bears from the feeding site. Nevertheless, simultaneous use of a feeding site by both polar and brown bears is a unique phenomenon and will be investigated further in the future.

Females with cubs spent less time feeding and more time laying, sitting, or standing in what might constitute vigilant behavior (Dyck and Baydack 2004). The protective nature of individual females may motivate them to avoid other cohorts, e.g. use the feeding sites during times of low bear density (day). However, frequent day visits to the feeding sites may simply be a result of cubs' higher energy demands needed for growth.

Use of Marine Habitat

Use of the Barter Island feeding site requires polar bears to enter marine waters to access and depart the site, unless they approach from the mainland, which was rarely observed. In addition to accessing the bone pile at Barter Island, polar bears also used marine waters for swimming and interacting. Family groups in particular spent more time in the water than other cohorts.

Movements and Interchange

Limited data from this study indicate that individual variability exists as to how long polar bears remain in the vicinity of the feeding sites. Some polar bears remained on site at both Barter and Cross islands for weeks at a time, and perhaps until freeze-up, whereas others remained only a few days. Duration of residence may be affected by environmental factors as well as by interactions with other bears and humans. No observations of polar bears using both Barter and Cross islands during our study periods were observed; however, telemetry data indicates that some interchange between the two islands can occur later in the season.

Whether or not the same bears use these feeding sites in subsequent years is also a subject for future study. Mauritzen (1999) found that female polar bears in the Norwegian Arctic exhibit some seasonal fidelity to certain habitat types, and that area fidelity was greater for near-shore individuals than for pelagic individuals. In Alaska, Amstrup et al. (2000) reported that, although activity areas for bears in the southern Beaufort Sea are large and variable, most included a "core area" of overlap each year. Of polar bears captured near Kaktovik during 1985-1994, 46% were re-observed there (Amstrup et al 2000). Other studies (Shideler and Wendling 2005) of brown bears on the North Slope report that many of the bears feeding at alternative food sources e.g. dumps, are the offspring of mothers that fed there as well. In fact, Shideler and Wendling (2005) found that all food-conditioned bears in the Prudhoe Bay oilfield area were related to one of two maternal "clans", one of which included three generations of bears that became conditioned to human food sources. All food-conditioned cubs (for which fate was known) became food-conditioned while with their mothers. Given these factors, there is a high probability that the number of polar bears, particularly at Barter Island, will increase in future years.

Management Applications and Future Research

Effective management of polar bears around human settlements requires knowledge of the number and age/sex classes of polar bears present, or likely to be present, over time. Results from this study are being used to monitor long-term trends of polar bear use of the Beaufort Sea coastline and for planning human activities such as oil and gas lease sales. In the future, however, scientists will need to better understand why polar bear use of coastal habitat is increasing, and more precisely what the role of alternative food sources such as marine mammal carcasses play in that trend. Previous studies indicate that polar bears can adapt to seasonal variation in ice and water conditions by making large-scale movements and increasing their home range size (Ferguson et al. 1999). Are changes in ice condition or food availability contributing to the increased use of coastal habitat in the Beaufort Sea? Is the presence of large males at the carcass sites an indicator of food stress in the marine environment? What is the overall contribution of whale remains to the energetic needs of polar bears? Future studies are needed to examine space-use patterns of individual polar bears to determine to what extent coastal use by polar bears is increasing, and to what extent the presence of bowhead whale carcasses are affecting that trend.

The study has also increased awareness to a growing concern over large numbers of bears concentrating near human developments, and the subsequent potential for increased bear-human conflicts. The Fish and Wildlife Service's goal is to minimize polar bear-human conflicts by minimizing polar bear-human interactions and decreasing bear densities in proximity to human settlements. Information obtained from this study will be used to guide management activities such as: 1) cooperative development of bear-human interaction plans with affected villages; 2) identifying options for minimizing attractants within and around human settlements; 3) increasing information and education on polar bear life history and the risks associated with increased bear use of coastal areas; and 4) structuring village-based polar bear patrols.

One of the primary concerns related to polar bear use of whale carcasses deposited near human settlements is to what extent polar bears are becoming food-conditioned to bowhead whale remains, namely, associating humans with a source of food. Past studies indicate that food-conditioned bears are most likely to pose a risk to humans (Herrero and Herrero 1997). A study is needed at Barter Island to follow specific polar bears and monitor their movements and behavior within and between years in relation to human settlements. Currently, scientists in

24

Alaska are investigating the use of Radio Frequency Identification (RFID) tags on polar and brown bears to track individual bears. If this technology proves successful, it could be used on Barter Island to: 1) identify and manage "problem" bears; 2) determine whether individual bears and their offspring return to Barter Island to feed on whale remains in subsequent years; and 3) more clearly evaluate the factors affecting the duration of residency of individual bears at Barter Island.

Finally, use of carcass remains along the coast of Alaska has also drawn attention to the potential for increased risk of disease transmission among both marine (polar bear) and terrestrial (grizzly bears, foxes, gulls) species when using the same food resources. Future studies are needed to address whether pathogens (viruses and protozoa) are present and being transmitted among polar bears and other species.

Literature Cited

Altmann, J. 1974. Observational study of behavior: sampling methods. Behavior 49(3-4): 227-267.

Amstrup, S. C. 2000. Polar Bear. Pp. 133-157 in J. J. Truett and S. R. Johnson, eds., the natural history of an Arctic oil field: development and the biota. Academic press, Inc. New York. 299pp.

Amstrup. S.C. and G.M. Durner, I. Stirling, N.J. Lunn, and F. Messier. 2000. Movements and distribution of polar bears in the Beaufort Sea. Can. J. Zool. pp.948-966.

Bentzen, T., E.H. Follmann, T.M. O'Hara, M.J. Wooler, S.C. Amstrup, and G.W. York. 2004. Trophic level differences among Alaskan polar bears inferred from nitrogen and carbon values. Poster presented at 15th International Conference on Bear Research and Management, San Diego, California.

Bureau of Land Management. 2005. Northeast National Petroleum Reserve - Alaska, final amended integrated activity plan/environmental impact statement, BLM/AL/PL-05/006, Anchorage, Alaska. 1610pp.

Durner, G.M., S.C. Amstrup, R. Neilson, and T. McDonald. 2004. The use of sea ice habitat by female polar bears in the Beaufort Sea. Minerals Management Service, OCS Study MMS 2004-014, Anchorage, Alaska. 41pp.

Dyck, M.G. and R.K. Baydack. 2004. Vigilance behaviour of polar bears (*Ursus maritimus*) in the context of wildlife-viewing activities at Churchill, Manitoba, Canada. Biol. Cons. 116: 343-350.

Ferguson, S.H, Taylor, M.K, Rosing-Asvid, A., Born, E.W., and Messier, F. 1999. Determinants of range size in polar bears. Ecological Letters 2:311-318.

Herrero, J. and Herrero, S. 1997. Visitor safety in polar bear viewing activities in the Churchill region of Manitoba, Canada. BIOS Environmental Research and Planning Associates, Ltd. Calgary, Alberta, Canada. 88pp.

Jacobson, M.J. and C. Wentworth. 1982. Kaktovik subsistence: land use values through time in the Arctic National Wildlife Refuge Area. U.S. Fish and Wildlife Service, Northern Alaska Ecological Services, report number NAES 82-01, Fairbanks, Alaska. pp. 3-5.

Kalxdorff, S.B. 1997. Collection of local knowledge regarding polar bear habitat use in Alaska. Technical Report MMM97-2, Marine Mammals Management, Anchorage, Alaska. 71pp.

Koski, W.R., J.C. George, G. Sheffield, and M.S. Galganaitis. 2005. Subsistence harvests of bowhead whales (*Balaena mysticetus*) at Kaktovik, Alaska, 1973-2000. J. Cetacean Res. Manage.7(1): 33-37.

Mauritzen, M., A.E. Derocher, and O. Wiig. 1999. Do female polar bears have home ranges? Poster presented at 13th Biennial Conference on the Biology of Marine Mammals, Wailea, Maui, Hawaii.

Schliebe, S., T. Evans, S. Miller, C. Perham, and J. Wilder. In Prep. Proceedings of 14th working meeting of the IUCN/SSC Polar Bear Specialist Group, 20-24 June 2005, Seattle Washington, U.S.A. U.S. Fish and Wildlife Service, Marine Mammals Management, Anchorage, Alaska (in U.S. Management section of Proceedings).

Shideler, R. and B. Wendling. 2005. Effects of food-conditioning on grizzly bears in the North Slope Oilfields: 2004 interim report. Unpubl. Rep. by Alaska Department of Fish and Game, Fairbanks, Alaska.

Smith, T.G. 1980. Polar bear predation of ringed and bearded seals in the land-fast sea ice habitat. Can. J. Zool. 58(12):2201-2209.

Stirling, I. 2002. Polar bears and seals in the eastern Beaufort Sea and Amundsen Gulf: a synthesis of population trends and ecological relationships over three decades. Arctic 55 (Supp.1): pp.59-76.

Stirling, I. and W.R. Archibald. 1977. Aspects of predation of seals by polar bears. J. Fish. Res. Board Can. 34:1126-1129.

Tacha, T.C., P.A. Vohs, G.C. Iverson. 1985. A comparison of interval and continuous sampling methods for behavioral observations. J. Field Ornithol. 56(3): 258-264.

U.S. Census Bureau. 2000. Population estimates for Kaktovik and Nuiqsut, Alaska, Census 2000, Washington DC.

U.S. Fish and Wildlife Service. 1995. Habitat conservation strategy for polar bears in Alaska.

Marine Mammals Management, Anchorage, Alaska. 232pp.

U.S. Fish and Wildlife Service. 1986. Arctic National Wildlife Refuge coastal plain resource assessment, final report: baseline study of the fish, wildlife, and their habitats. Region 7, Alaska, v. 1, section 1002C, pp. 289-295.

Personal Communications and Unpublished Data

Craig George, North Slope Borough Department of Wildlife Management, Barrow, Alaska: data regarding polar bear aggregations near Point Barrow, Alaska provided to S. Miller, 2005.

North Slope Borough, Department of Wildlife Management, Barrow, Alaska: data regarding bowhead whale harvests on the North Slope provided to S. Miller, 2005.

Michael Galginaitis, Applied Sociocultural Research, Anchorage, Alaska: personal communication with S. Miller, 2005.

Schliebe, Scott: U.S. Fish and Wildlife Service, Marine Mammals Management, Anchorage, Alaska.

Shideler, Richard, Alaska Department of Fish and Game, Fairbanks, Alaska: personal communication with S. Miller, 2005.

TEK 2005: Traditional ecological knowledge collected from residents of Kaktovik and Nuiqsut, Alaska, regarding polar bear use of marine mammal carcasses. Unpublished data, Marine Mammals Management, Anchorage, Alaska.

U.S. Geological Survey, Alaska Science Center: Polar Bear Database information provided to S. Miller, 2004-2005.

Appendix 1. Field Data Collection Definitions

Age/Sex Classification

Age	Sex	Dependents
Adult (A) = > 5 years old	Male (M)	Cub of the year (COY) = <1 year old
Sub-adult (S) = 2.5-5 years old	Female (F)	Yearling (Y) = 1-2.5 year-old
Unknown (U) = unknown age	Unknown (U) = unknown sex	N/A = no dependent animals

Behavior/Activities

Sitting (si) resting (r) attentive (a) comfort (c) grooming (g)	Laying (la) resting (r) sleeping (s) comfort (c) grooming (g)	Standing (st) attentive (a) comfort (c) grooming (g)	Walking (wk)	Running (ru)
Feeding (fe) whale (w) kill (k) snow/ice (s) herbaceous (h) urine (u) other (o)	Interacting (in) play (p) aggressive (ag) fight (f) neutral (n) submissive (s) other (o)	Interacting Family (if)	Playing (pl)	Swimming (sw)
Rolling (ro)	Urination (ur)	Defecation (df)	Unobservable (uo)	Other (ot)

Definitions

Sitting: body positioned on haunches
      resting - eyes open but not focused on stimuli
      attentive - alert; focused on a perceived stimulus
      comfort - scratching, rubbing, or stretching body
      grooming - using tongue, snow, water, or ice to lick body
Laying: body positioned prone on ground on either belly, back or side
      resting - same as above
      sleeping - eyes closed and not reacting to stimuli
      comfort - same as above
      grooming - same as above
Standing: body positioned on either hind or all four legs
      attentive - same as above
      comfort - same as above
      grooming - same as above
Walking: moving on all four legs at a slow pace
Running: moving at a trot or lope on all four legs
Feeding: ingesting food, including biting, chewing, swallowing, and/or looking for food (short bouts of < 1minute of moving and/or sniffing with head lowered to the ground while in close proximity (10 m) of food source; includes carrying food in mouth

whale - whale carcass
kill - fresh kill (note species)
herbaceous - plant material
snow/ice - snow or ice
urine - animal urine
other - anything not listed above
Interacting: subject interacting with another bear(s) outside its family group
play - non-aggressive social interaction; play fighting
Aggressive - dominant social display such as huffing or charging without contact with other bear(s)
Fight - aggressive social interaction involving contact with another bear(s)
Neutral - social interaction that involves posturing or other non-aggressive or submissive displays
Submissive - social interaction that results in subject retreating away from other bear(s)
Interacting family: adult female polar bear interacting with her dependent cubs; includes nursing
Playing: handling an object
Swimming: moving through water with feet not touching the bottom surface; if wading, classify as walking but change habitat code to "open water" (see below)
Rolling: moving from side to side with body in contact with the ground
Urination: releasing a liquid bowel movement
Defecation: releasing a solid bowel movement
Unobservable: out of view of the observer(s)
Other: anything not included above (describe in notes)

Habitat Types

Open water (**OW**) = marine environment
Shorefast ice (**SH**) = shore-fast ice attached to the mainland or barrier islands
Pack ice (**PI**)= unconsolidated active pack ice such as ice pans or bergs
Barrier Island (**BI**) = land surrounded on all sides by water; includes all of Cross Island and Bernard Spit
Mainland (**MA**) = land attached to the Coastal Plain; includes Barter Island
Unknown (**UH**) = unknown habitat type

Habitat types within the study area were defined as: mainland (Barter Island feeding site and all visible areas except Bernard Spit and open water), barrier island (Cross Island, Bernard Spit), or open water (non-terrestrial marine areas).